Sound Trackers

Rock and Rap

SOUND TRACKERS – ROCK AND RAP
was produced by

David West ☖ Children's Books
7 Princeton Court
55 Felsham Road
London SW15 1AZ

Series Concept: Bob Brunning
Designer: Rob Shone
Picture Research: Fiona Thorne
Editor: Ross McLaughness

First published in Great Britain in 2002 by
Heinemann Library, Halley Court, Jordan Hill, Oxford OX2 8EJ, a division of
Reed Educational and Professional Publishing Limited.

OXFORD MELBOURNE AUCKLAND
JOHANNESBURG BLANTYRE GABORONE
IBADAN PORTSMOUTH (NH) USA CHICAGO

06 05 04 03 02
10 9 8 7 6 5 4 3 2 1

ISBN 0 431 09115 3 (HB)
ISBN 0 431 09122 6 (PB)

British Library Cataloguing in Publication Data

Pickering, James
Rock and rap. - (Soundtrackers)
1. Rock music - Juvenile literature
2. Rap (Music) - Juvenile literature
3. Rock musicians - Juvenile literature
4. Rap musicians - Juvenile literature
I. Title
781.6'6

Rock and Rap

James Pickering

Heinemann
LIBRARY

CONTENTS

On these discs is a selection of the artist's recordings. Many of these albums are available on CD. If they are not, many of the tracks from them can be found on compilation CDs.

These boxes give you extra information about the artists and their times.
Some contain anecdotes about the artists themselves or about the people who helped their careers or, occasionally, about those who exploited them.
Others provide historical facts about the music, lifestyle, fans, fads and fashions of the day.

Super Furry Animals were recently voted Wales's best band.

INTRODUCTION

Rap is a vocal style, which has dominated urban American music for over 20 years. In the late 1970s, young DJs discovered they could borrow, or 'sample', excerpts of recordings, and stitch them together to make a new song. Add some spoken or shouted lyrics (rap), and you have a new type of music. Rappers competed to come up with wittier and more rebellious lyrics. The first rap hit was 'The Message' by Grandmaster Flash and the Furious Five in 1982. Dozens of acts followed, venting their frustrations and obsessions in rap – poverty, politics, drugs and crime.

Grandmaster Flash samples records, spinning or scratching two discs at once.

Influenced by rap, heavy metal, grunge and dance music, legions of white bands emerged in the mid-'90s, playing nu-metal, hardcore rap, post-grunge, rap-metal, industrial metal – take your pick. These styles of music are as much about attitude as music. Provocative lyrics and maximum volume combine with an image of tattoos, dyed hair and pierced bodies to cause hysteria among teenagers, and outrage among their parents! Many rock and rap stars have ended up in court, owing to their violent lifestyles – which just makes them seem even more glamorous to some fans.

In Britain, rock bands, such as the Manic Street Preachers, are hardly short on attitude, fired by the same anger as their American counterparts. Other stars, such as Fatboy Slim, are exploring gentler territory, influenced by the rave scene which swept the country in the '90s.

EMINEM

The most talented and witty rapper to come out of
America in the 1990s? Or a precocious and offensive
product of the white establishment, who makes a living
out of making enemies? The choice is yours. Whatever
you think of him, Eminem was the biggest-selling rapper
to emerge at the turn of the new millennium. He has an
infamous reputation, even amongst those who have no
interest in modern music.

DOCTOR'S APPOINTMENT

Marshall Mathers, or Eminem (M 'n' M),
was 23 years old, homeless and broke
when he accepted an invitation to
perform at the 1997 Rap
Olympics in Los Angeles. He
sorely needed the $500 prize
money, but despite a
rapturous welcome by the
mainly black and Hispanic
crowd, he only came
second. Bitterly
disappointed, Eminem was
preparing for the lonely
journey home, when he was
approached by two talent
scouts from Interscope
Records. After listening to a
tape of Eminem's music,
Interscope arranged an
appointment with the doctor – Dr Dre,
the chief figure in West coast rap music.

CAUSING A STIR

The colour of his skin led several less talented rappers to view Eminem with suspicion, but Dre had no such doubts. He signed Eminem, and they immediately began work on the 'Slim Shady' album, which was a huge hit, helped by the singles 'My Name Is' and 'Guilty Conscience'. But Eminem's violent and foul-mouthed lyrics stirred up controversy in the media. The single 'Stan' was targeted for its graphic description of an obsessive and homicidal fan, though it made a star out of Dido, whose voice was featured on the track.

Eminem was fined for weapons offences in 2001.

GUILTY OR NOT GUILTY?

No stranger to the courts, Eminem has faced firearms and assault charges, and has even been sued by his ex-wife and his mother! Just before a concert tour of his country in 2001, Australian Prime Minister John Howard said that Eminem's songs are 'sickening, demean women and encourage violence'. But Eminem insists that his lyrics are strictly tongue-in-cheek, and he is only trying to cause debate, not offence.

DOCTOR IN THE HOUSE

Dr Dre is the godfather of West coast gangsta rap music, which often contains violent and obscene lyrics. Along with Ice Cube, he was a member of the rap group NWA. His first solo album was called 'The Chronic', and it was a huge hit. He went on to produce the controversial rapper Snoop Doggy Dogg, between spells in prison. Dre also founded the rap record labels Death Row and Aftermath.

Dr Dre gave $1,000,000 to charity, following the American terrorist attacks in 2001.

'Slim Shady' 1999

'The Marshall Mathers LP' 2000

Eminem's mother sued him for comments he made about her on his records.

7

FATBOY SLIM

Talk about a versatile star! Norman Cook, from Bromley, has been in the music business for nearly 20 years, during which time he has played bass guitar in a pop group, produced other artists, recorded samples and remixes, worked as a club DJ and created his own new electronic sounds. Today, he records under the name of Fatboy Slim, the most popular of the new breed of 'Brithop' dance producers.

ONE BAND TO THE NEXT

Norman joined Hull-based four-piece the Housemartins in 1986, and played bass with the band until they split the following year. He then returned to the South of England, to record with Beats International. They hit No. 1 with 'Dub Be Good To Me', but this was yet another short-lived collaboration. It looked as though everything Norman touched turned to gold – his next project was with the 'acid jazz' act Freak Power, whose 'Tune In, Turn On, Drop Out' single hit No. 2.

'Better Living Through Chemistry' 1996
'On The Floor At The Boutique' 1998

'You've Come A Long Way Baby' 1998
'Halfway Between The Gutter And The Stars' 2000

MAN OF MANY PARTS

Norman's ambition was to enter the record books by scoring the most top 40 hits under different names. He worked as a producer and DJ under the names Pizzaman, Fried Funk Food, Might Dub Katz and Norman Cook Presents Wildski. His latest incarnation is Fatboy Slim.

The Housemartins were well known for their left wing political views.

RECORD BREAKER

Norman Cook achieved his ambition when Fatboy Slim's 'Going Out Of My Head' entered the chart in 1997. Tracks from Fatboy Slim's first album became club anthems, and Norman threw himself into his work, remixing Jean-Jacques Perrey's single 'Eva' and Cornershop's 'Brimful Of Asha', which spent several weeks at No. 1. American success came with his second album, which provided the hit singles 'The Rockafeller Skank' and 'Praise You'.

SCREEN STAR

Many Fatboy Slim tracks have ended up on film soundtracks or in television commercials, which have yielded Norman Cook a large fortune. He now works from home by the sea in Brighton. His music has been given a further boost by his work with Spike Jonze, who directed the video of 'Weapon Of Choice', starring Christopher Walken, which won an amazing six MTV Video Music Awards in September 2001.

Norman married the TV and radio presenter Zoe Ball in 1999. They have a young son called Woody.

THE ART OF DJing
To be a successful club DJ takes years of practice, skill and imagination. DJs need technical know-how and an instinctive feel for the music and their audience. While a record blares from the speakers into one ear, DJs line up other discs on separate turntables, listening with headphones on the other ear. These days, some club DJs are as famous as the musicians whose records they play.

DJs create 'scratching' effects, by spinning records with their hands.

www.BRITs.co.uk

FOO FIGHTERS

Only rarely do drummers in major bands enjoy successful solo careers after their bands have split up. It's even more rare for a drummer to start a new band, which is just as big as the one he has left. But Dave Grohl is no ordinary drummer.

SNUFFED OUT

Nirvana was the biggest band of the early 1990s, with singer and guitarist Kurt Cobain at the helm, and Dave Grohl on drums. Dave had been playing drums, guitar and writing songs since his early teens, and had found long-awaited fame with Nirvana. But the band was in trouble, and it was clear to everyone close to it that Kurt Cobain was suffering from mental problems, made worse by his addiction to drugs. In early 1994, he committed suicide, and the band that had re-written rock history was no more.

On stage with Foo Fighters, Dave Grohl plays guitar and sings.

WORD OF MOUTH

After several months of silence following Kurt's death, Dave booked some studio time with his old friend Barrett Jones. Dave had a large backlog of songs, and the two of them recorded an entire album in just a week, playing all the instruments themselves. Dave made 100 cassette copies of the new album, giving them to friends and associates in the music business. Word of the tape spread like wildfire, and before he knew it, record companies were frantically bidding against each other to release the album.

'Foo Fighters' 1995
'The Colour And The Shape' 1997

'There Is Nothing Left To Lose' 1995

OUT OF THIS WORLD

In the meantime, Dave recruited a band, which he named Foo Fighters, after a World War Two special force, who investigated UFOs. Capitol Records signed them, and released Dave's solo recordings under the group name, even though none of the rest of the band had played on them. The album was an instant success in America, spearheaded by the radio-friendly hit single 'This Is A Call'.

WALK-OUTS

Dave did what he knew best, and hit the road with his new band, touring throughout 1996. Late that year, Foo Fighters began sessions for their second album, but quarrels led to the departure of drummer William Goldsmith, leaving Dave to pick up the sticks himself. 'The Colour And The Shape' was the first album Foo Fighters recorded as a band, although there would be more resignations – guitarist Pat Smear left soon after its release, and his replacement also proved short-lived. Foo Fighters recorded their third album as a trio, Dave's songwriting skills surviving any number of line-up changes.

NIRVANA

Dave Grohl joined Nirvana in 1990, fresh from the punk band Scream. Nirvana was formed in Seattle, and typified the 'grunge' sound that came out of that city. Grunge was a raw mixture of angry and tortured lyrics, thunderous drumming and blaring guitars. Millions of teenage fans sympathised with Kurt Cobain's bleak view of the world, and almost felt that he was writing about their own experiences. A decade later, Nirvana is still an enormous influence on the nu-metal bands of today.

Kurt Cobain married the singer from Hole, Courtney Love. They had a daughter together.

Foo Fighters are influenced by the punk scene of the late 1970s.

LIMP BIZKIT

Who says that rock stars shouldn't play businessman? With his angry look, tattooed limbs and burly physique, Fred Durst is the face of 'rapcore' – a mix of hip-hop, heavy metal and punk. But Fred is also a video director, scriptwriter, and a record company executive, in charge of millions of dollars' worth of talent.

'Three Dollar Bill Y'All' 1997
'Significant Other' 1999

'Chocolate Starfish
And The Hot Dog Flavored Water' 2000

ALL AT SEA

Fred Durst had an unhappy childhood – he was bullied at school, partly because his fascination with black rap culture made him stand out from the crowd. Fred's stepfather, who had fought in the Vietnam War, was strict with him, and in an attempt to please him, Fred joined the US Navy when he left school. Life at sea didn't suit Fred at all, and he bitterly regretted his mistake. Out of uniform, he drifted between casual jobs, finally becoming a tattooist, while he developed an early version of Limp Bizkit, in his hometown of Jacksonville, Florida. One day, Fieldy, the bass-guitarist with Korn, entered Fred's tattoo parlour, and rolled up his sleeve.

TATTOO AND A TAPE

Limp Bizkit headlined the Family Values Tour in 1999.

As well as several tattoos, Fieldy gained Fred's friendship, and was happy to accept a cassette of Limp Bizkit's early recordings. The other members of Korn were so impressed that they passed the tape on to their producer Ross Robinson, who helped to secure Limp Bizkit a support slot on tour with House of Pain and the Deftones. Record companies vied to sign the band, and in 1998 Flip/Interscope released their debut album, which turned them into the most talked-about act on the rapcore scene.

THE DARK SIDE

The follow-up, 'Significant Other' entered the US chart at No. 1, and sold 4,000,000 copies in its first six months. All the while, Fred Durst was proving himself a clever businessman, snapping up senior positions at the Flip and Flawless labels. But there was a dark side to this massive success. Limp Bizkit stirred up controversy at the 1999 Woodstock Festival, which culminated in riots. Although the band played the day before the worst of the violence, there were reports of rapes and numerous injuries during Limp Bizkit's set, and much of the media accused Fred of egging the crowd on to cause trouble.

Fred Durst worked as a gardener and shop assistant after leaving the Navy.

NOT TO BE MESSED WITH

Fred Durst can be a forceful character, who has sometimes clashed with his tourmates. He was also a supporter of the controversial Napster website, which allowed fans to trade music over the Internet – depriving performers and record companies of royalties. Limp Bizkit were back in 2000, with a new album, and a triumphant tour.

Limp Bizkit played free concerts on a tour sponsored by Napster.

KORN
The Californian band Korn helped Limp Bizkit on their way in the early part of their career. Korn emerged in the wake of Nirvana, playing 'funk-metal', and became one of the most provocative and popular bands of the mid-1990s. Korn made headlines in 1998, when a young student was sent home from school by his disgusted head teacher, for wearing a T-shirt adorned with the band's logo.

Korn's biggest album was 'Issues', released in 1999.

MANIC STREET PREACHERS

Wales has given the world some astonishing bands over the last few years, none more so than the Manic Street Preachers. Their rebellious attitude, heavy guitar rock and dangerous image made them darlings of the music press. But the Manics also had to overcome the tragedy of losing one of their key members.

'Generation Terrorists' 1992
'Gold Against The Soul' 1993
'The Holy Bible' 1994

'Everything Must Go' 1996
'This Is My Truth Tell Me Yours' 1998
'Know Your Enemy' 2001

START OF THE JOURNEY

For a group which once proclaimed that all bands should break up after releasing just one album, the Manics have lasted a long time! The band was formed in Blackwood, Wales in 1988, featuring James Dean Bradfield on vocals and guitar, Nicky Wire on bass guitar, Sean Moore on drums, and later, the band's driver, Richey Edwards, also on guitar. The band gained a reputation for its stunning live performances, and Manics' singles 'Motown Junk' and 'You Love Us' prompted plenty of press adulation.

James Dean Bradfield and drummer Sean Moore are cousins.

TORTURED SOUL

Richey Edwards caused a sensation in 1991 when he sparked an argument with a music journalist, who had questioned the band's originality. Richey produced a knife, and carved the word '4Real' on to his own arm. Many people dismissed this as a publicity stunt, but it was in fact an early indication of Richey's mental instability. The Manics' first top 10 hit was a version of 'Suicide Is Painless', the theme to the TV comedy series 'M*A*S*H'. By 1993, it was clear that Richey was suffering from alcoholism, anorexia and depression, which culminated in more acts of self-mutilation. He once appeared on stage with chest injuries, which he had given himself with knives a fan had given him. In 1994, he entered a private clinic, to try to rid himself of his demons.

James Dean Bradfield plays a Gibson Les Paul guitar.

The Manics say they miss Richey Edwards most on stage.

WELSH ROCKERS

For years, Wales was more associated with middle-of-the-road singers, such as Tom Jones and Shirley Bassey, than hard rock music. But in the last few years, a wealth of talent has come out of the principality. As well as the Manics, Wales has given us Stereophonics, Super Furry Animals and Catatonia, who sadly announced their split in September 2001. The popular singer and songwriter David Gray was born in Manchester, but has lived in Wales for most of his life.

Cerys Matthews (second from left) was the flamboyant lead singer with Catatonia.

MISSING PERSON

The Manics' third album 'The Holy Bible' was a bleak and sombre record, but this didn't stop them winning over even more fans. Richey briefly rejoined his bandmates, but the news they had been dreading finally came in February 1995. Richey vanished, leaving behind his passport and credit cards. A week later his car was found near the Severn Bridge, a notorious suicide spot – he has never been seen since. Bravely, the band decided to carry on, using the lyrics Richey left behind. The Manics went from strength to strength, establishing themselves as superstars all over the world, although, like many British acts of the day, American success eluded them. Always a controversial band, in 2001 they became the first western act to play for the hard-line communist dictator of Cuba, Fidel Castro.

MARILYN MANSON

As long ago as the late 1960s, certain rock musicians adopted ghoulish images and flirted with the idea of devil-worship, or Satanism. But Marilyn Manson was the first major star openly to embrace Satanism, calling himself the 'Antichrist Superstar'. He is certainly an American anti-hero, who has won over millions of fans, while enraging parents and conservative public opinion.

TRUE ORIGINAL?

Cynical rock critics often compare Manson with Alice Cooper, the '70s star who still dons zombie-like make-up and sings of pestilence and death, even though he is a respectable golf-playing family man these days! Like Alice Cooper, Marilyn also adopted a girl's name.

LONE WOLF

But while Alice Cooper's act is humorous, Manson seems serious in his beliefs. Brian Warner always considered himself an outcast as a youth, until he found a soulmate in guitarist Scott Mitchell. They formed a band in Tampa Bay, Florida in 1989, with Warner changing his name to Marilyn Manson, and Scott Mitchell to Daisy Berkowitz.

SPOOKY MUSIC

Marilyn Manson and the Spooky Kids became well-known for their elaborate make-up and homemade special effects. They found a friend in Trent Reznor of Nine Inch Nails, who offered them a contract with his record label, and a support slot on his next tour. They didn't need asking twice! The group increased its fanbase at every show, as word of mouth spread about their outrageous singer.

Marilyn Manson's band has seen a number of line-up changes.

ROCK IN THE DOCK

As well as Marilyn Manson, many metal acts have been accused of experimenting with the occult, including Black Sabbath and Led Zeppelin, although both acts deny the charge. Judas Priest were accused of putting hidden messages on their record 'Stained Class', which drove two fans to shoot themselves. The fans' American families took the band to court, though the case collapsed almost immediately.

Judas Priest suffered the indignity of having to perform their songs in court.

INTENDING TO OFFEND

Marilyn Manson sealed his reputation in Salt Lake City, home of the Mormon religion. He tore up a copy of the Mormons' Holy Book on stage, and was given the title 'Reverend' by the Church of Satan's founder. Marilyn Manson's shows have been picketed by religious activists ever since. A master of self-publicity, many people still accuse Marilyn of being a showbiz sell-out, particularly since the publication of his best-selling autobiography, 'The Long Hard Road'. But supporters of free speech praise him for his bravery. In an age where rock sets out to shock, Marilyn Manson is surely the most controversial star to emerge over the last few years.

Manson's fans are mostly urban, white teenage boys.

'Portrait Of An American Family' 1994
'Smells Like Children' 1995
'Antichrist Superstar' 1996

'Mechanical Animals' 1998
'Last Tour On Earth' 1999
'Holy Wood' 2000

MASSIVE ATTACK

Massive Attack were the pioneers of 'trip-hop' music, a smooth mix of hip-hop rhythms, melodic tunes and samples. The band was also one of the most influential groups of its day, and paved the way for other acclaimed acts, such as Portishead, Sneaker Pimps, Tricky and Beth Orton.

WILD NIGHTS

Massive Attack evolved from the Wild Bunch, which formed in 1983 on the Bristol club scene. They astounded clubbers with the way they could move effortlessly between musical styles as varied as punk, soul and reggae, and their shows were so popular that bands playing in other parts of town found they were performing to empty halls.

FALSE START

The Wild Bunch folded in the mid 1980s, but two members, Adrian 'Mushroom' Vowles and Grant 'Daddy G' Marshall hooked up with Robert '3D' del Naja to form Massive Attack. Three years later, they released their first single, 'Daydreaming', featuring the cool vocals of Shara Nelson, and the rapper Tricky. The music press heaped praise on Massive Attack, particularly the single 'Unfinished Sympathy', which remains a club favourite to this day. But their early records never sold in huge quantites, and after an unfulfilling American tour, it looked as if the band might not survive.

3D is also a graffiti artist, whose work has been exhibited in galleries.

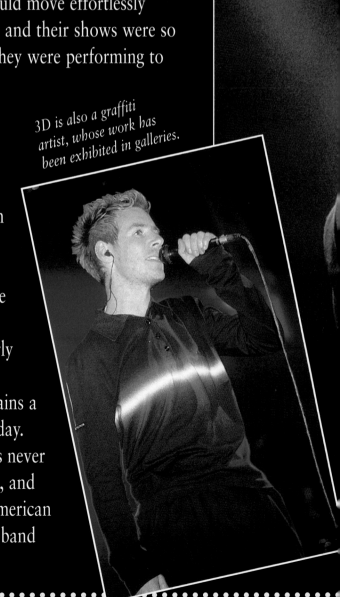

'Blue Lines' 1991
'Protection' 1994

'Mezzanine' 1998
'Singles 90/98' 1999

FAME AND RESPECT

Massive Attack took three years to lick their wounds, before the release of 'Protection' in 1994. The band has always been rated by fellow musicians as one of Britain's finest dance/rap outfits, and U2, Garbage and Madonna all jumped at the chance to collaborate with them. They shared the band's philosophy that good dance music must also be fun just to listen to. Massive Attack's fans are a patient lot! The band only releases albums every few years, but every one is well worth the wait.

MICROCHIP MUSIC

Today, anyone with a few pieces of simple hardware and software can make music in their own home. You don't need to be an instrumental virtuoso to cut a CD – by sampling excerpts of other people's records you can create a new one of your own. But is sampling a legitimate artform, or just a lazy way of stealing other people's ideas? The debate rages on.

A computer can enable anyone to make electronic music anywhere, from a concert hall, to a club, to a bedroom.

Massive Attack briefly abbreviated their name to Massive in the early 1990s.

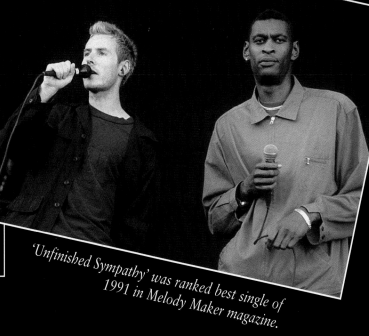

'Unfinished Sympathy' was ranked best single of 1991 in Melody Maker magazine.

OFFSPRING

Californian band the Offspring was one of the biggest 'post-grunge' bands to emerge after Nirvana. 'Smash' sold over four million copies after its independent release in 1994.

THE SKATE SCENE
Skateboarding is an important part of the rock and rap culture, but the sport has been around for longer than you might imagine. It was first invented in California in the 1960s, by frustrated surfers who wanted something to do on the days when they couldn't get out to sea. Today there are skate parks in many towns, where skateboarders can practise tricks, such as the kickflip, ollie, nollie, varial, indy and nose grab.

The Offspring's music, and that of similar bands, has been called 'skate punk'.

'Offspring' 1989
'Ignition' 1993
'Smash' 1994

'Ixnay On The Hombre' 1997
'Americana' 1998
'Conspiracy Of One' 2000

MODERN METAL

The Offspring's music is often described as 'punk-pop', although the group probably owes more to gritty, guitar-led heavy metal. Guitarist Kevin 'Noodles' Wasserman's powerful riffs perfectly complement Dexter Holland's almost expressionless vocals. The band first came to light in 1989, and released a couple of low-key albums, which won them some local success. The big break came with their album 'Smash', including the single 'Come Out And Play', which became a big hit on MTV and radio. Offers from major labels flooded in, but the Offspring stayed loyal to its small indie label – for a while at least!

The Offspring toured the States in 2001.

MUSIC ON THE NET

Eventually, the financial lure proved too strong and the band left their label, Epitaph, and attracted criticism from some of the bands they left behind. The Offspring annoyed their new bosses at Sony, by announcing in 2000 that they intended to offer their new album to fans, to download free of charge on the Internet – a plan which was scrapped when Sony threatened to sue.

PAPA ROACH

Success rarely comes overnight in the music business, but Papa Roach had to wait longer than most for their first hit. The band formed at high school in California in 1993, but it was seven years before a major record label released one of their albums.

ALTERNATIVE METAL

The original members of Papa Roach were Coby Dick, Jerry Horton, Dave Buckner and Will James. Soon after forming, they started making short recordings of their own songs, which were dubbed 'alternative metal', to distinguish them from the traditional heavy metal of the 1970s and '80s. Change arrived in 1996, when Will was replaced by their 16-year-old roadie, Tobin Esperance, and a new manager encouraged them to release a full-length album.

'Infest' 2000

'Maximum Papa Roach' 2001

DREAM COMES TRUE

Local radio stations picked up on 'Old Friends From Young Years', and the album became a surprise minor hit. The band hit the road, sharing the stage with Suicidal Tendencies, Sevendust and Powerman 5000. A record deal with Dreamworks led to their major-label debut. 'Infest' finally gave them the success they had craved, and Papa Roach spent the next two years playing to ever-larger audiences.

Papa Roach appeared, along with Marilyn Manson, at the 2001 Ozzfest festival.

THE PRODIGY

Keith Flint of the Prodigy is one of the most recognisable faces in Britain, which is remarkable, because dance acts tend to shun the limelight. The Prodigy's decision to focus on their image, as well as their music, saw them cross into the mainstream pop charts, to become the biggest 'electronica' act of the 1990s.

COTTAGE INDUSTRY

The origins of the Prodigy were in producer Liam Howlett's Essex bedroom in the late 1980s. Liam set up his own studio at home, and came up with 'What Evil Lurks', which was a big hit on the rave scene in 1990. Keith Flint and Leeroy Thornhill were regulars on the scene and they linked up with Liam to form the Prodigy. The band was unusual from the start, mixing the atmosphere of a rave, with the sort of showmanship more associated with arena rock bands.

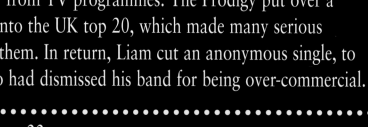

Keith Flint (right) combines a pierced body with a punk hairstyle.

DANCING UP THE CHARTS

In fact, Liam hardly changed the Prodigy's sound, from their earliest efforts, right through to their world famous records, five years later. He mixed fierce metal chords with aggressive chanted vocals from Keith, sampling brief spoken words, usually from TV programmes. The Prodigy put over a dozen singles into the UK top 20, which made many serious clubbers reject them. In return, Liam cut an anonymous single, to fool the DJs who had dismissed his band for being over-commercial.

'Experience' 1992
'Music For The Jilted Generation' 1995

'The Fat Of The Land' 1997
'Experience Expanded' 2001

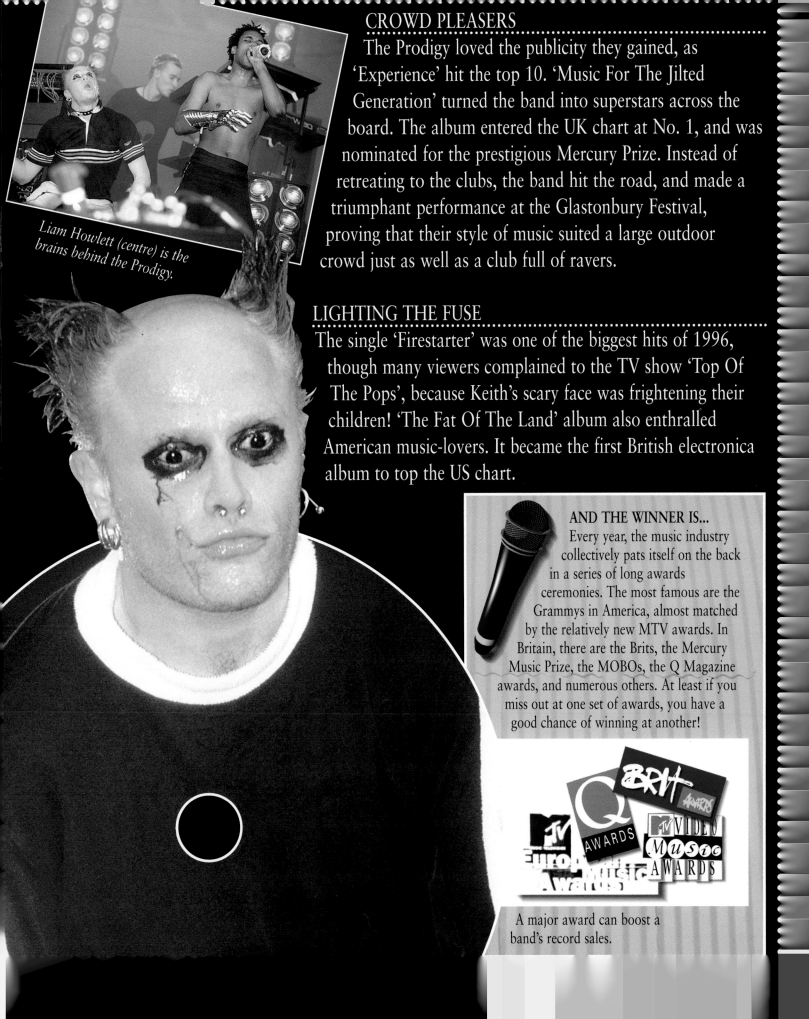

Liam Howlett (centre) is the brains behind the Prodigy.

CROWD PLEASERS

The Prodigy loved the publicity they gained, as 'Experience' hit the top 10. 'Music For The Jilted Generation' turned the band into superstars across the board. The album entered the UK chart at No. 1, and was nominated for the prestigious Mercury Prize. Instead of retreating to the clubs, the band hit the road, and made a triumphant performance at the Glastonbury Festival, proving that their style of music suited a large outdoor crowd just as well as a club full of ravers.

LIGHTING THE FUSE

The single 'Firestarter' was one of the biggest hits of 1996, though many viewers complained to the TV show 'Top Of The Pops', because Keith's scary face was frightening their children! 'The Fat Of The Land' album also enthralled American music-lovers. It became the first British electronica album to top the US chart.

AND THE WINNER IS...

Every year, the music industry collectively pats itself on the back in a series of long awards ceremonies. The most famous are the Grammys in America, almost matched by the relatively new MTV awards. In Britain, there are the Brits, the Mercury Music Prize, the MOBOs, the Q Magazine awards, and numerous others. At least if you miss out at one set of awards, you have a good chance of winning at another!

A major award can boost a band's record sales.

PUFF DADDY

In 1993, Sean 'Puffy' Combs started working from home as a remixer. A decade later, he is in charge of a multi-million dollar entertainment empire, and has produced records for Craig Mack, Notorious B.I.G., Boyz II Men, Mariah Carey, TLC and Lil' Kim. He is also a fine rapper in his own right, releasing material under the name Puff Daddy.

Puffy was briefly a dancer before he joined Uptown Records.

GOING IT ALONE

Born in the New York borough of Harlem, the young Sean was a bright boy who eventually attended university in Washington D.C. An old friend, Heavy D, worked at Uptown Records and found Sean a traineeship there. Within months, he was an executive, with ambitions to be a vice president of the company. But when Puffy was fired from his job, he decided to go it alone, and set up his own company, Bad Boy Entertainment.

SUCCESS TURNS SOUR

A year of hard work gave Bad Boy its first big hit, when Puffy's remix of Craig Mack's 'Flava In Ya Ear' hit the top 10. Notorious B.I.G.'s 'Big Poppa' did even better, but as Bad Boy got bigger, it became involved in a bitter feud with the West coast label Death Row. Tupac Shakur, Death Row's biggest star, mocked Puffy and B.I.G. in one of his videos, and accused Puffy of being involved in a shooting. In 1996, Tupac was himself shot dead by an unknown killer, and just six months later, B.I.G. met the same fate, just before his second album, 'Life After Death', hit No. 1.

TRIBUTE

Puffy was distraught, but after a break he returned as Puff Daddy with 'Can't Nobody Hold Me Down', which held the US No. 1 slot for two months. But his biggest hit was yet to come – 'I'll Be Missing You', a heartfelt tribute to B.I.G., featuring his widow Faith Evans.

IMAGE CHANGE

Soon after, Puff Daddy found himself in trouble with the law, when he was arrested for allegedly firing a gun in a nightclub, then fleeing the scene. He faced the prospect of a hefty jail sentence, but was acquitted, though one of his associates was found guilty. Recently he has been in more trouble, mostly for traffic offences. Puffy has tried to shed his bad boy image, adopting a more mature, business-like persona. He has even changed his nickname to P. Diddy, to distance himself from his past.

'No Way Out' 1997
'Forever' 1999

'P. Diddy & The Bad Boy Family:
The Saga Continues' 2001

THE DARK SIDE OF RAP

Rap lyrics are often violent and obscene. They can also express a vicious hatred for women, white people, the police – in fact almost anyone. 'Gangsta rap' can often spill over into real gang culture, as the murders of B.I.G. and Tupac demonstrated. But not all rap is so full of anger. Will Smith is a huge rap star who does not use bad language on his records, and Public Enemy supported rap's 'Stop The Violence' movement in the late 1980s.

Notorious B.I.G. was also known as Biggie Smalls.

Puffy's Bad Boy empire is worth hundreds of millions of dollars.

RED HOT CHILI PEPPERS

The Red Hot Chili Peppers are a revolving door of a rock band. Members have been and gone, returned and died, ever since they formed in 1983. They were ahead of their time – one of the first bands to mix punk, funk, rap and metal into an intense brand of heavy rock. It took a few years for the music business to catch up with them.

SCHOOL BUDDIES
Michael 'Flea' Balzary, Hillel Slovak and Jack Irons played in a band together at high school. Anthony Kiedis was a fan, who used to open their shows by reciting poetry, and gradually became part of the band. News of their performance at a drug-fuelled party spread like wildfire, and within six months, they had an eight album deal with EMI.

IN AND OUT
The band gained a reputation for its outrageous stage shows, which they often performed virtually nude! The first major line-up change came before the band's first album was even released – Hillel and Jack departed, to be replaced by Jack Sherman and Cliff Martinez. In early 1984, Sherman was out of the band, and Hillel was back in, and in 1985, Martinez was dumped to be replaced by Jack Irons, the drummer he had replaced. Confused? So were the Chilis – their heavy drug-taking and rigorous life on the road were affecting their judgement, and threatening the survival of the band.

Anthony Kiedis (above) has admitted to serious drug problems in the past. He cut his hair and dyed it blond in the late 1990s (right).

'Red Hot Chili Peppers' 1984
'Freaky Styley' 1985
'Uplift Mofo Party Plan' 1987
'Mother's Milk' 1989

'Blood Sugar Sex Magik' 1991
'What Hits!?' 1992
'One Hot Minute' 1995
'Californication' 1999

DOWN AND OUT

Most worryingly, Hillel was sliding into a life of heroin addiction, and although the Chilis' records were beginning to sell in large quantities, on stage, he often forgot the notes, and let the rest of the band down. A decision was made to fire Hillel, but, in typical Chilis fashion, they changed their mind. It was hardly surprising when Hillel fatally overdosed in 1988, but the band was badly shaken. Worst affected was Jack Irons, who left the group.

BACK AGAIN

After a break, the band reconvened, with John Frusciante on guitar, and finally entered the premier league of rock with 'Blood Sugar Sex Magik'. But in 1992, Frusciante was out, and after several replacements had come and gone, Dave Navarro settled into the job. The Chilis were plagued by ill-health and traffic accidents in the 1990s. Flea and Navarro joined Jane's Addiction, and after a brief tour, Navarro decided not to return to the Chilis. John Frusciante was back in the band for 'Californication' and the tour that followed it. Whose turn is it to leave next?

JANE'S ADDICTION
Dave Navarro joined the Chilis from Jane's Addiction, one of the most unusual bands to emerge in the mid-1980s. Fronted by the flamboyant frontman Perry Farrell, the band combined pure rock with metal, punk, folk and even jazz music. Jane's Addiction split in 1991, but invited Navarro and Flea to join their reunion in 1997. Afterwards, Navarro realized that he never wanted to tour again and left the Chilis for good.

Perry Farrell used to design his band's album covers.

SHAGGY

Shaggy is the biggest star of contemporary reggae music, following in the footsteps of such greats as Bob Marley and Lee Perry. But Shaggy doesn't sing tortured songs of resistance, like other reggae greats – his style veers from pop and R&B to good-time dancehall tunes, and back to reggae again, making him a favourite with a huge range of music fans. And he got his break in music while he was in uniform.

'Pure Pleasure' 1993
'Boombastic' 1995

'Midnite Lover' 1997
'Hotshot' 2000

MILITARY MAN

Orville Richard Burrell was born in Kingston, Jamaica in 1968. He was nicknamed Shaggy by friends, after the greedy character in the 'Scooby Doo' TV cartoon. When he was 18, Shaggy joined his mother in Brooklyn, New York, and decided to pursue a career in music. He hit No. 1 on the reggae charts with 'Mampie' and 'Big Up', but the hits soon dried up. Frustrated by his lack of mainstream success, Shaggy enlisted with the US Marines.

LIVE ON STAGE

Many samplers and rappers are only used to making music in studios or small clubs. When it comes to playing in large arenas, they often leave the audience cold. Like the Prodigy, Shaggy has mastered the art of showmanship – combining great singing, with energetic dancing to reach out to his audience. As Shaggy himself has said, 'if you don't know me yet, come to a Shaggy concert. I guarantee, when you leave, you'll be a Shaggy fan!'

Shaggy has played to crowds all over the world.

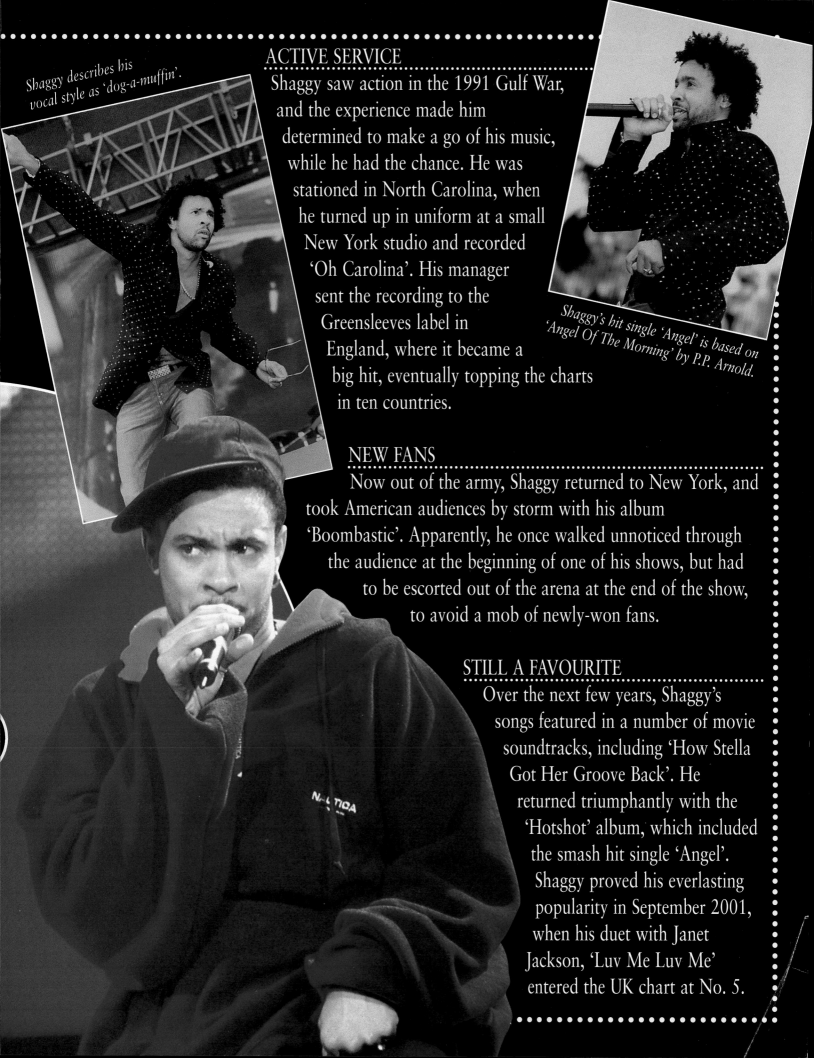

Shaggy describes his vocal style as 'dog-a-muffin'.

ACTIVE SERVICE

Shaggy saw action in the 1991 Gulf War, and the experience made him determined to make a go of his music, while he had the chance. He was stationed in North Carolina, when he turned up in uniform at a small New York studio and recorded 'Oh Carolina'. His manager sent the recording to the Greensleeves label in England, where it became a big hit, eventually topping the charts in ten countries.

Shaggy's hit single 'Angel' is based on 'Angel Of The Morning' by P.P. Arnold.

NEW FANS

Now out of the army, Shaggy returned to New York, and took American audiences by storm with his album 'Boombastic'. Apparently, he once walked unnoticed through the audience at the beginning of one of his shows, but had to be escorted out of the arena at the end of the show, to avoid a mob of newly-won fans.

STILL A FAVOURITE

Over the next few years, Shaggy's songs featured in a number of movie soundtracks, including 'How Stella Got Her Groove Back'. He returned triumphantly with the 'Hotshot' album, which included the smash hit single 'Angel'. Shaggy proved his everlasting popularity in September 2001, when his duet with Janet Jackson, 'Luv Me Luv Me' entered the UK chart at No. 5.

GAZETTEER

Modern musical trends change so quickly that it's sometimes difficult to keep up with them. With so many Limp Bizkit and Nirvana imitators out there, 'alternative rock' is no longer alternative. Time for the trend-setters to start thinking up some new names for the music!

Green Day stole the show at the 1994 Woodstock Festival, which helped sales of their album 'Dookie'.

Chris Frantz and Tina Weymouth of the Tom Tom Club also contribute to Gorillaz.

Feeder's bass guitarist, Taka Hirose (left) was born in Tokyo, Japan.

POST GRUNGE

Along with Pearl Jam, Green Day was the biggest post-Nirvana grunge band. Their album 'Dookie' sold eight million copies. Feeder led the British post-grunge scene with their albums 'Polythene' and 'Yesterday Went Too Soon'.

BEHIND THE MASK

Sometimes musicians like to hide from the limelight. Damon Albarn of Blur leaped at the chance to perform in the 'virtual hip-hop' act Gorillaz, whose members are computer-animated characters. The first Gorillaz album, 'Tomorrow Comes Today' appeared in 2000, and fans can keep up with the imaginary band on its website. Linkin Park has been dubbed a nu-metal boy band, partly because their first album, 'Hybrid Theory' appealed to young pop fans and contained no swearing.

Linkin Park shared the stage with Papa Roach at the 2001 Ozzfest festival.

Nobody could possibly call Slipknot a boy band. Their aggressive, masked stage act has taken rap-metal to new extremes.

GENTLY DOES IT

Placebo's music is often described as 'neo-glam', harking back to 1970s acts, such as T. Rex and David Bowie. Their back-to-basics 2001 album 'Black Market Music' won over many mainstream rock fans. Wheatus have also attracted many older fans, who have no interest in other post-grunge bands.

Founded by brothers Brendan and Peter Brown, Wheatus released their first album in 2000.

Slipknot's Corey Taylor does his best to scare the pants off his audiences!

Placebo performed at glam rock star David Bowie's 50th birthday.

RAP'S OLD-TIMERS

The Beastie Boys are veterans of the rap scene. They were the first white rap act to be taken seriously by black audiences and rappers. The boys caused outrage when they first appeared in the 1980s, and many countries tried to ban them from their shores. But today, the rap veterans are held in great affection as they turn up at rock festivals every summer.

'Licensed To Ill' is the Beastie Boys' best-known album.

Brendan Brown sings and plays guitar in Wheatus. His brother Peter plays drums.

INDEX

PHOTOGRAPHIC CREDITS *Abbreviations: t-top, m-middle, b-bottom, r-right, l-left, c-centre.*
Cover m, bm, br, 10 both, 11b & br, 12br, 13br, 14 both, 15m & mr, 16 both, 17tm, 18 both, 20bl, 21tr, 22 both, 23 both, 26m, 28 both, 28-29b, 30br (Mick Hutson) Cover bl, 9bl, 24bl & mr (JM Enternational) 3, 27tr, 31bl (Ebet Roberts) 4-5, 30mr (Benedict Johnson) 5tr (Simon King) 6tl, 7br, 9br, 18-19b, 20tl, 26br, 29 both, 31tr & br - (Nicky J. Sims) 6bl (Simon Ivan) 7tm (Nigel Crane) 7mr, 8b, 15bl (George Chin) 8tl (Patrick Ford) 9tr, 13tr, 19br (Paul Bergen) 11mr, 13tm, 17br, 21b, 31tl (Grant Davis) 12tl, 27b (Sue Schneider) 17mr (Fin Costello) 24tl (Paul Fenton) 25mr (Des Willie) 25br (Salifu Idriss) 26tl (Michel Linssen) 30tl (Robert Knight) - Redferns.